Digital Defenders

The Consultant's Guide to Cyber Risk Management

Table of content

Preface 1

    The Need for Cybersecurity Today 1
    Target Audience 1
    How to Use This Book 2

Chapter 1: Introduction to Cybersecurity 3

    Background and Evolution 3
    Importance in the Modern World 3
    Major Cyber Attacks: A Brief Overview 4

Chapter 2: Understanding Digital Assets 7

    Defining Digital Assets 7
    Categorizing Assets: Personal vs. Corporate 7
    Importance of Digital Assets in Various Industries 8

Chapter 3: Basics of Risk Management 11

    The Concept of Risk 11
    Risk Assessment vs. Risk Management 11
    The Lifecycle of Risk Management 12

Chapter 4: Assessing Risks in the Digital Realm 15

    Identifying Vulnerabilities and Threats 15
    Risk Assessment Tools and Techniques 16
    Understanding the Impact and Likelihood 16
    Calculating Risk 17

Chapter 5: Key Principles of Mitigating Risks 19

    Defense in Depth 19

    The Principle of Least Privilege 19

    Incident Response Planning 20

    Regular Audits and Reviews 20

Chapter 6: Technological Strategies for Risk Management 23

    Firewall and IDS/IPS Systems 23

    Encryption and Key Management 24

    Secure Coding Practices 24

    Patch Management 25

Chapter 7: Human Factors in Cybersecurity 27

    Social Engineering Attacks 27

    Security Awareness Training 27

    Insider Threats 28

    Building a Cybersecurity Culture 28

Chapter 8: Legal and Regulatory Aspects of Cybersecurity 31

    Global Cybersecurity Standards and Laws 31

    The Role of Regulatory Compliance 31

    Implications for Cybersecurity Consultants 32

Chapter 9: Being a Cybersecurity Consultant 35

    Required Skillsets and Qualifications 35

    Building a Portfolio and Gaining Experience 35

    Ethical Considerations 36

    Continual Learning and Certification 36

Chapter 10: Case Studies in Cybersecurity 39

    Analysis of Major Cybersecurity Incidents 39

    Lessons Learned 39

    How a Consultant Could Make a Difference 40

TABLE OF CONTENT

Chapter 11: Future Trends in Cybersecurity 41
Rise of Quantum Computing and its Implications 41
Increasing Automation in Cybersecurity 41
The Role of AI and Machine Learning 42

Chapter 12: Building a Cybersecurity Practice 45
Structuring a Consultancy Business 45
Collaborative Tools for Cybersecurity Teams 45
Marketing and Client Acquisition Strategies 46

Conclusion 49
Reflection on the Changing Cybersecurity Landscape 49
Encouraging Proactivity in Risk Management 50

Appendices 51
A: Glossary of Cybersecurity Terms 51
B: Recommended Reading and Resources 54
C: List of Important Cybersecurity Conferences and Forums 56
D: Tools and Software Recommendations for Consultants 58
Index 61

Preface

The Need for Cybersecurity Today

In today's interconnected world, the boundaries between the physical and digital have blurred. As we've integrated technology into nearly every aspect of our lives and businesses, the potential for cyber threats has skyrocketed. Daily headlines of data breaches, ransomware attacks, and other cyber incidents serve as a grim reminder of the challenges we face. The safety of our data, financial assets, and even our personal privacy is at stake. This has propelled the need for skilled cybersecurity professionals and consultants to the forefront. The aim of this book is to guide those individuals in navigating the vast seas of cybersecurity risks and defenses.

Target Audience

This book is crafted for:

1. **Aspiring Consultants**: Individuals eager to dive into the world of cybersecurity consulting, providing expert guidance to businesses and organizations.
2. **Current IT Professionals**: Those already in the tech field, seeking to pivot or expand their expertise into cybersecurity risk management.
3. **Business Leaders**: Executives and managers wanting to understand the cyber risks their enterprises face and seeking guidance on best practices.
4. **General Readers**: Anyone curious about the digital threats of today and wishing to be better informed.

Regardless of your current knowledge level, this guide is designed to offer a structured pathway through the complexities of cybersecurity risk management.

How to Use This Book

The journey through "Risk Management in Cybersecurity: A Consultant's Guide" is structured to be both intuitive and comprehensive.

- **Begin with Basics**: Start with the foundational concepts of digital assets and risk management. Grounding yourself in these basics ensures you're well-prepared for the more advanced topics ahead.

- **Engage with Real-World Scenarios**: Through various case studies, see how theoretical knowledge applies in real-world situations. These instances are invaluable for practical understanding and application.

- **Utilize Tools and Resources**: As you progress, you'll encounter tools, techniques, and resources. While they serve as reference points, they're also there to bolster your hands-on expertise.

- **Reflect and Revisit**: The cybersecurity landscape is dynamic. Regularly revisit sections, especially those on upcoming trends, to stay updated.

As you delve into the subsequent chapters, always remember the core goal: to not only understand risk but to manage and mitigate it. With this guide, you'll be well-equipped to do just that. Welcome to the realm of Digital Defenders.

CHAPTER 1:

Introduction to Cybersecurity

Background and Evolution

Cybersecurity, at its core, is about protecting systems, networks, and data from digital attacks. However, the realm of cybersecurity wasn't born overnight. As technology advanced, so did the threats.

In the early days of computing, security was a concern limited to academics and larger institutions. The first computer viruses were often more about mischief than malice. Fast forward to the rise of the internet, and the game changed dramatically. Connecting millions of devices globally, the internet became a breeding ground for various threats. From viruses to worms, the challenges started growing in scale and sophistication.

Today, cybersecurity isn't just about preventing nuisance attacks. It's a discipline dedicated to safeguarding national security, businesses, and individual privacy.

Importance in the Modern World

Digitalization has transformed our world. From online banking to remote work, our reliance on digital systems is unparalleled. This heavy dependence on technology, while convenient, also presents significant risks. Cyber threats today can:

1. **Compromise Personal Data**: Identity theft is more common than we'd like to admit, with individuals finding their personal details sold on the dark web.
2. **Hurt Businesses**: Beyond monetary losses, businesses can suffer reputational damage that takes years to rebuild following a cyber attack.
3. **Impact National Security**: Cyber espionage and warfare are real threats, with nation-states involved in cyber operations against one another.

In essence, cybersecurity is no longer an optional luxury; it's a critical necessity.

Major Cyber Attacks: A Brief Overview

The importance of cybersecurity is further underscored when we look at some of the most significant cyber attacks in history:

- **WannaCry Ransomware Attack (2017)**: Using a Windows vulnerability, the WannaCry ransomware spread across 150 countries, crippling hospitals, businesses, and home users alike.
- **Equifax Data Breach (2017)**: A major credit bureau, Equifax, was hit by a breach that exposed the personal data of 147 million people, highlighting the risks associated with holding vast amounts of sensitive data.
- **Sony Pictures Hack (2014)**: Beyond just data theft, this attack had geopolitical implications. Allegedly orchestrated by North Korea, the hack showcased how cyber attacks could be used as a form of political coercion.

These are just a few instances from a long list of cyber incidents. Each underscores the dire need for robust cybersecurity measures.

In conclusion, as we forge ahead in this digital age, understanding the foundations and significance of cybersecurity becomes pivotal. This chapter sets the stage for a deeper dive into risk assessment, management, and mitigation in the subsequent sections. As the digital landscape continues to evolve, so must our strategies to protect and defend it.

CHAPTER 2:

Understanding Digital Assets

Defining Digital Assets

At its core, a digital asset is any data, be it text, images, multimedia content, or any other digital file, that holds value. In a world where interactions, transactions, and records are increasingly digital, these assets play a pivotal role. They could be as simple as a digital photograph, as personal as an individual's health records, or as complex as a company's intellectual property.

In more technical terms, digital assets can be seen as data which, when stored, processed, and disseminated, offers tangible or potential value to the owner. Their worth comes from their utility, uniqueness, or the data they encapsulate.

Categorizing Assets: Personal vs. Corporate

Digital assets often vary in nature, depending on the context. Let's delve into two broad categories:

1. **Personal Digital Assets**:

- **Digital Media**: This includes photographs, videos, and even social media posts.
- **Personal Documents**: E-books, tax records, health histories, and other personal digital documents fall here.

- **Digital Identity**: Information related to one's online identity, including login credentials, email archives, and more.

2. **Corporate Digital Assets**:

- **Intellectual Property**: Patents, trade secrets, and proprietary software, among others.
- **Business Records**: Financial reports, customer databases, and employee records.
- **Digital Products**: Software products, mobile applications, or any other digital goods offered by the business.
- **Online Presence**: Websites, official social media profiles, and related content.

It's crucial to note that the boundaries between personal and corporate digital assets can sometimes blur, especially in the age of remote work or with personal devices being used for corporate tasks.

Importance of Digital Assets in Various Industries

Every industry, in some way, is intertwined with the world of digital assets. Their importance cannot be understated:

- **Healthcare**: Patient records, treatment histories, and research data are all digital assets. Their confidentiality, accuracy, and availability can directly impact patient care.
- **Finance**: For banks and financial institutions, digital assets include transaction records, account details, and trading algorithms. A breach could be catastrophic, leading to financial losses and a shattered reputation.
- **Entertainment**: Here, digital assets might be movie scripts, songs, or entire films. Unauthorized leaks or piracy can result in significant revenue loss.

- **Retail and E-commerce**: Digital assets include customer databases, product catalogs, and transaction histories. Their safety ensures smooth business operations and customer trust.
- **Manufacturing**: Designs, blueprints, and proprietary processes are vital digital assets. Their theft can give competitors an undue advantage.
- **Education**: Digital teaching materials, research papers, and student records are key assets in the educational sector.

This list is by no means exhaustive. The universality of digital assets across industries highlights their central role in today's economy.

In summary, digital assets are the lifeblood of the modern digital age. Recognizing their value and understanding their nature is the first step towards formulating effective cybersecurity strategies. As we move on, we'll delve deeper into the risks these assets face and how to shield them effectively.

CHAPTER 3:

Basics of Risk Management

The Concept of Risk

At its most basic, risk denotes the potential for loss or harm when pursuing a particular action or inaction. In the context of cybersecurity, risk relates to the potential harm or damage that could arise due to vulnerabilities in digital systems when faced with various threats. This could be a data breach due to unpatched software, financial loss from a cyberattack, or reputational damage following a security incident.

Understanding risk isn't merely about acknowledging threats but also weighing them against the potential rewards or benefits. For example, introducing a new software might speed up company operations (a reward), but it could also introduce vulnerabilities (a risk).

Risk Assessment vs. Risk Management

While the terms 'risk assessment' and 'risk management' are sometimes used interchangeably, they have distinct meanings:

1. **Risk Assessment**:
   - **Purpose**: To identify and evaluate risks. This means recognizing potential threats, determining the vulnerabilities they might exploit, and gauging the potential damage.
   - **Process**: Typically, it involves:

- **Identification**: Recognizing potential threats and vulnerabilities.
- **Evaluation**: Estimating the likelihood of a threat exploiting a vulnerability and the potential impact.

2. **Risk Management**:

- **Purpose**: To make informed decisions about how to address the identified risks. This could involve accepting, avoiding, mitigating, or transferring the risk.
- **Process**: Key steps include:
- **Risk Response**: Deciding how to address each risk based on its assessment.
- **Implementation**: Putting in place measures to manage risks, such as security protocols or insurance policies.
- **Monitoring and Review**: Continually observing the managed risks and adapting strategies as necessary.

While risk assessment provides a snapshot of current risks, risk management is an ongoing process of addressing and revisiting those risks.

The Lifecycle of Risk Management

Risk management isn't a one-off task. It's a continuous cycle that evolves with the threat landscape and the organization's objectives. Here's a simplified breakdown of the risk management lifecycle:

1. **Identification**: Recognizing potential threats and vulnerabilities. This could be new malware in the wild or emerging tech in the company that could be exploited.
2. **Assessment**: Evaluating the potential consequences and likelihood of each risk.
3. **Response Strategy**: Formulating a plan on how to tackle each identified risk.
4. **Implementation**: Enacting the chosen risk response strategies.

5. **Monitoring**: Keeping an eye on the effectiveness of risk management measures and the emergence of new threats or changes in existing ones.
6. **Review and Revise**: Regularly reassessing the risk landscape, the effectiveness of current measures, and tweaking strategies as required.
7. **Report and Inform**: Keeping stakeholders, whether they're top management or individual users, informed about risks and the measures in place.

This lifecycle ensures that risk management is dynamic, adapting to the ever-changing digital landscape.

In conclusion, risk management is the bedrock of effective cybersecurity. By understanding what risks are, how they're assessed, and the processes to manage them, organizations stand a better chance against the myriad of cyber threats. As we progress, we'll delve deeper into specific strategies and tools that make this process more efficient and effective.

CHAPTER 4:

Assessing Risks in the Digital Realm

Identifying Vulnerabilities and Threats

Every digital ecosystem, whether it's a simple personal device or a sprawling corporate network, has its weak points or vulnerabilities. These are essentially the gaps or flaws that can be exploited. When matched with threats (entities or situations with the potential to cause harm), they formulate the core of our digital risk landscape.

1. **Vulnerabilities**: They can be:

- **Software-based**: Outdated software, unpatched systems, or insecure code.

- **Hardware-based**: Physical points of entry like USB ports or inherent design flaws.

- **Human**: Employees falling for phishing schemes or using weak passwords.

2. **Threats**: Ranging from hackers to malware, from insider threats to natural disasters, these are entities or events with the potential to exploit vulnerabilities.

Understanding the landscape means knowing where you might be weak and what's out there trying to take advantage.

Risk Assessment Tools and Techniques

In the vast digital realm, manual risk assessment can be cumbersome. Thankfully, several tools and techniques can aid this process:

1. **Vulnerability Scanners**: Software tools that scan systems to identify known vulnerabilities.
2. **Penetration Testing**: Simulated cyberattacks on systems to identify vulnerabilities from an attacker's perspective.
3. **Threat Modeling**: Systematically identifying threats by examining each component of a system and determining potential vulnerabilities.
4. **Phishing Simulations**: Testing employees' awareness by simulating phishing attacks.

Using a combination of these tools and techniques provides a comprehensive view of the risk landscape.

Understanding the Impact and Likelihood

Two critical components determine the gravity of a risk: its potential impact and its likelihood of occurrence.

1. **Impact**: This gauges the potential damage a realized threat can cause. Impact can be financial, reputational, operational, or any combination thereof.
2. **Likelihood**: This assesses how probable it is for a threat to exploit a vulnerability. Not every vulnerability will be targeted, and not every threat is likely to materialize.

Together, understanding impact and likelihood helps prioritize which risks need urgent attention.

Calculating Risk

With a clear view of vulnerabilities, threats, impact, and likelihood, the next step is risk calculation. In its most basic form, risk can be calculated as:

$Risk = Impact \times Likelihood$

While this formula offers a simplified view, in practice, risk assessment tools might use more complex algorithms accounting for multiple variables. The end goal, however, remains the same: to quantify risk in a way that it can be ranked, prioritized, and subsequently managed.

In conclusion, assessing risks in the digital realm is a blend of understanding the environment, employing the right tools, and a systematic approach to gauging threats and vulnerabilities. With a clear risk assessment, organizations can move from reactive stances to proactive strategies, ensuring a safer digital future. As we progress through the book, we'll explore how to use this assessment to formulate robust risk management strategies.

CHAPTER 5:

Key Principles of Mitigating Risks

Defense in Depth

Often referred to as the "layered approach," defense in depth is a strategy that doesn't rely on a single security measure to protect digital assets. Instead, it employs multiple layers of defense to ensure that even if one layer is breached, others remain intact.

1. **Physical Security**: This can be as straightforward as locked doors to server rooms or surveillance cameras.
2. **Network Security**: Involves firewalls, intrusion detection systems, and secure network architectures.
3. **Computer Security**: This includes antivirus software, end-point protection, and patch management.
4. **Application Security**: Involves regular updates, secure coding practices, and penetration testing.

Think of defense in depth as a castle with its moats, walls, gates, and guards. Each layer has its role, ensuring that the castle remains secure.

The Principle of Least Privilege

The principle of least privilege (PoLP) dictates that any user or system process should only have access to the resources absolutely necessary for its legitimate purpose and nothing more. This reduces the potential damage from accidents or breaches.

1. **User Access**: Employees should only access data and applications pertinent to their job role.
2. **System Processes**: Systems and applications should run with the least permissions necessary, minimizing potential damage if compromised.

By strictly adhering to PoLP, even if an attacker gains access to a particular user's credentials, the damage they can inflict is limited.

Incident Response Planning

While the goal is to prevent incidents, it's equally vital to be prepared for them. An incident response plan (IRP) is a structured approach detailing the processes to follow when a cybersecurity incident occurs.

1. **Preparation**: Setting up the necessary tools, teams, and strategies before an incident.
2. **Detection**: Recognizing and acknowledging the breach or incident.
3. **Containment**: Limiting the scope and magnitude of the incident.
4. **Eradication**: Removing the cause of the incident.
5. **Recovery**: Restoring and validating system functionality.
6. **Lessons Learned**: Documenting the incident, analyzing it, and implementing measures to prevent future occurrences.

A well-structured IRP ensures swift action, reducing potential damage and restoring normalcy as quickly as possible.

Regular Audits and Reviews

Continuous evaluation and adaptation are paramount in the ever-evolving landscape of cybersecurity. Regular audits and reviews serve this purpose:

1. **Security Audits**: Systematic evaluations of security measures to ensure they're up-to-date and effective.

2. **Risk Reviews**: Periodic reassessments of the risk landscape, accounting for new threats and vulnerabilities.
3. **Policy Reviews**: Revisiting organizational security policies to ensure they're in line with the current environment.

These reviews ensure that risk mitigation strategies remain relevant and robust against emerging challenges.

In conclusion, mitigating risks isn't about a singular action but a combination of well-established principles and continuous efforts. Embracing these principles ensures that organizations remain a step ahead of potential threats, safeguarding their invaluable digital assets. As we move forward, we'll delve deeper into specific strategies and technologies that amplify these principles.

CHAPTER 6:

Technological Strategies for Risk Management

Firewall and IDS/IPS Systems

Firewalls and Intrusion Detection/Prevention Systems (IDS/IPS) are the first line of defense against unwanted intruders.

1. **Firewalls**: Acting as gatekeepers, they control incoming and outgoing network traffic based on a set of security rules.

   - **Benefits**: Protects against unauthorized access, filters malicious web traffic, and segregates different segments of the network.

2. **IDS/IPS**: While similar, there's a slight difference between the two.

   - **Intrusion Detection Systems (IDS)**: Monitors network traffic and alerts administrators to suspicious activities.

   - **Intrusion Prevention Systems (IPS)**: Actively blocks or prevents identified suspicious activities.

   - **Benefits**: Offers real-time protection, detects known and unknown threats, and aids in rapid response to potential breaches.

Together, firewalls and IDS/IPS form a robust barrier, scrutinizing and managing the data that flows in and out of networks.

Encryption and Key Management

Encryption translates data into a code to prevent unauthorized access. Key management, on the other hand, involves handling cryptographic keys that unlock this encrypted data.

3. **Encryption**: Useful in various scenarios such as:

- **Data at Rest**: Protecting stored data, like databases or files.
- **Data in Transit**: Safeguarding data as it travels over the internet or between devices.

4. **Key Management**: Ensures that the cryptographic keys are:

- **Stored Securely**: Often in hardware security modules or secure key storage solutions.
- **Rotated Regularly**: Periodically changing keys to reduce the risk of exposure.
- **Accessible Only to Authorized Users**: Protecting keys from both external and internal threats.

By encrypting data and managing keys effectively, organizations can ensure the confidentiality and integrity of sensitive information.

Secure Coding Practices

Applications and software, while central to many operations, can be a prime target for cyberattacks. Secure coding practices ensure these are built with security in mind.

1. **Input Validation**: Ensures that only properly formatted data enters the system, preventing injection attacks.
2. **Authentication and Authorization**: Confirming the identity of users and granting access only to the necessary resources.
3. **Error Handling**: Preventing error messages from revealing too much about the system, which could aid attackers.

4. **Regular Code Reviews**: Periodically reviewing code to identify and rectify potential vulnerabilities.

Secure coding practices act as a preemptive measure, ensuring applications are robust against a wide range of threats.

Patch Management

Software, no matter how securely coded, can have vulnerabilities. Patch management involves the systematic deployment of updates to fix these vulnerabilities.

1. **Regular Monitoring**: Staying informed about new patches released for software in use.
2. **Testing**: Before full deployment, patches should be tested in a controlled environment to ensure they don't introduce new issues.
3. **Deployment**: Once tested, patches are rolled out across the organization.
4. **Verification**: Confirming that patches have been successfully applied and are functioning as intended.

Effective patch management reduces the window of opportunity for attackers, ensuring systems remain updated and resilient against known vulnerabilities.

In conclusion, a robust risk management strategy in the digital realm leans heavily on the right technology. By deploying and managing these technological tools and strategies effectively, organizations can erect formidable defenses against the myriad of threats they face. In subsequent chapters, we'll discuss the human element of risk management and the role of organizational culture in fostering a secure environment.

CHAPTER 7:

Human Factors in Cybersecurity

Social Engineering Attacks

While technology remains at the forefront of cybersecurity, humans often prove to be the most vulnerable point of attack. Social engineering exploits this vulnerability, manipulating individuals into divulging confidential information or performing certain actions.

1. **Phishing**: Emails masquerading as trustworthy entities, aiming to steal sensitive data.
2. **Pretexting**: Creating fabricated scenarios (pretexts) to extract information from victims.
3. **Tailgating**: Unauthenticated individuals gaining physical access by following authorized personnel.

Recognizing these tactics is the first step to defense. Being skeptical, verifying requests, and being aware of unsolicited communications can help thwart such attacks.

Security Awareness Training

Empowering individuals with knowledge is crucial in cybersecurity. Proper training helps employees recognize and respond to threats.

1. **Regular Workshops**: Updating staff about the latest threats and safe online practices.

2. **Simulated Attacks**: Testing employee awareness by simulating phishing attacks or other threat scenarios.
3. **Feedback and Learning**: After simulations, provide feedback, and reinforce learning points.

Continuous training ensures that as cyber threats evolve, the human element of an organization evolves alongside in defense.

Insider Threats

Not all threats come from the outside. Sometimes, the threat is within—disgruntled employees, careless staff, or even those with malicious intent.

1. **Accidental Insiders**: Well-meaning employees who unintentionally cause security breaches, often due to lack of knowledge or oversight.
2. **Malicious Insiders**: Individuals within the organization who deliberately harm the company, whether for personal gain, revenge, or other motivations.

Addressing insider threats involves a mix of technical measures, like access controls, and organizational measures, such as employee well-being programs and regular monitoring.

Building a Cybersecurity Culture

A truly secure organization goes beyond tools and policies. It fosters a culture where every individual understands the importance of cybersecurity and acts on it.

1. **Leadership Commitment**: Senior management should lead by example, emphasizing the importance of security.
2. **Open Communication**: Encourage employees to voice concerns, report suspicious activities, and seek clarifications on security protocols.

3. **Rewarding Awareness**: Recognize and reward employees who actively participate in maintaining security, whether by identifying potential threats or suggesting improvements.

When cybersecurity becomes part of the organizational DNA, it transforms from a set of guidelines into a lived experience for every member.

In conclusion, the human factor, often termed the "weakest link" in cybersecurity, can be transformed into a formidable line of defense. By understanding human vulnerabilities, offering the right training, addressing internal threats, and fostering a security-first culture, organizations can greatly bolster their security posture. The subsequent chapters will delve deeper into integrating these human-focused strategies with technological solutions for a holistic approach to cybersecurity.

CHAPTER 8:

Legal and Regulatory Aspects of Cybersecurity

Global Cybersecurity Standards and Laws

With the interconnected nature of the digital realm, it's essential to recognize that cybersecurity isn't just about technological defenses—it's also governed by a tapestry of laws and standards.

1. **International Standards**: Documents like ISO/IEC 27001 provide guidelines on information security management, applicable globally.
2. **Regional Laws**: Areas like the European Union have introduced regulations such as the General Data Protection Regulation (GDPR) which mandates strict data protection measures.
3. **Country-Specific Legislation**: Individual countries often have their own set of cybersecurity laws tailored to their specific needs and concerns.

Understanding and adhering to these laws and standards is crucial for organizations operating in the digital space, both to maintain trust and to avoid legal complications.

The Role of Regulatory Compliance

While the multitude of regulations might seem daunting, they play a pivotal role in shaping the cybersecurity landscape.

1. **Setting a Baseline**: Regulations provide a minimum standard of security measures that organizations must implement.
2. **Protecting End-Users**: By ensuring that companies adhere to specific security standards, regulations aim to protect the data and rights of users.
3. **Penalties and Incentives**: Regulatory bodies often have the power to impose sanctions on non-compliant organizations, incentivizing them to prioritize cybersecurity.

It's imperative that businesses view compliance not just as a mandatory requirement but as an integral component of their cybersecurity strategy.

Implications for Cybersecurity Consultants

As a cybersecurity consultant, understanding the legal and regulatory environment is paramount.

1. **Advisory Role**: Consultants need to guide organizations in navigating the complex landscape of cybersecurity laws and standards, ensuring they remain compliant.
2. **Staying Updated**: The legal realm of cybersecurity is dynamic. Consultants must stay abreast of changes to provide accurate and timely advice.
3. **Risk Assessment**: Apart from technological vulnerabilities, consultants should also identify legal vulnerabilities, ensuring clients understand potential legal risks and take necessary precautions.

In essence, a consultant's role is multifaceted, intertwining technological expertise with a deep understanding of the legal framework.

In conclusion, the legal and regulatory aspects of cybersecurity provide a structured framework that guides and mandates security practices. It's not merely about technology but the broader societal implications of data protection, user rights, and organizational responsibilities. As we venture further, we'll explore the integration of these legal considerations with hands-on cybersecurity practices, aiming for a cohesive, all-encompassing approach to digital security.

CHAPTER 9:

Being a Cybersecurity Consultant

Required Skillsets and Qualifications

Stepping into the shoes of a cybersecurity consultant demands a unique blend of technical know-how and soft skills.

1. **Technical Proficiency**: A deep understanding of IT infrastructure, networking, encryption, and other core tech areas is fundamental.
2. **Analytical Mindset**: Ability to dissect complex problems, identify vulnerabilities, and devise solutions is crucial.
3. **Communication Skills**: Translating complex technical jargon into understandable terms for clients ensures successful collaboration and understanding.

The combination of these skills forms the foundation for a successful consultant, making them both technically competent and approachable.

Building a Portfolio and Gaining Experience

Credentials on paper are vital, but real-world experience distinguishes top-tier consultants from the rest.

1. **Starting Small**: Early in one's career, taking on smaller projects or internships can help in garnering experience.
2. **Case Studies**: Documenting past projects, challenges faced, and solutions implemented can act as testament to your expertise.

3. **Networking**: Building relationships within the industry can open doors to new opportunities and collaborations.

Each project and interaction adds to a consultant's repertoire, enhancing credibility and expertise.

Ethical Considerations

In the realm of cybersecurity, ethics isn't just a buzzword—it's a responsibility.

1. **Client Confidentiality**: Maintaining the secrecy of client data and information is paramount.
2. **Transparency**: Clearly communicating potential conflicts of interest or limitations in one's expertise ensures trust.
3. **Integrity**: Offering honest assessments and recommendations, even if they don't align with a client's initial preferences, upholds the consultant's role as a trusted advisor.

Operating within a framework of ethics solidifies a consultant's reputation and ensures long-term success in the field.

Continual Learning and Certification

The world of cybersecurity is ever-evolving. For consultants, staying stagnant isn't an option.

1. **Certifications**: Earning certifications like CISSP, CISM, or CEH showcases a commitment to staying updated and deepens expertise in specific areas.
2. **Workshops and Conferences**: Participating in industry events provides insights into the latest trends and innovations.
3. **Peer Collaboration**: Engaging with fellow professionals can provide new perspectives and solutions to shared challenges.

Dedication to continual learning ensures consultants remain at the forefront of their field, ready to tackle the cybersecurity challenges of today and tomorrow.

In conclusion, being a cybersecurity consultant is more than just understanding the intricacies of digital security. It's about being a trusted and ethical guide, always ready to learn and adapt, with a clear commitment to safeguarding the digital realm. As our exploration into cybersecurity continues, future chapters will delve into more advanced topics and strategies, building on the foundational knowledge established so far.

CHAPTER 10:

Case Studies in Cybersecurity

Analysis of Major Cybersecurity Incidents

Case studies provide invaluable insights into the practical challenges and consequences of cybersecurity breaches. Let's delve into a couple of notable incidents:

1. **Equifax Data Breach (2017)**: This incident compromised the personal information of nearly 147 million people. An unpatched vulnerability in a web application was the entry point for hackers, leading to one of the largest data breaches in history.
2. **WannaCry Ransomware Attack (2017)**: A global cyberattack by the WannaCry ransomware cryptoworm targeted computers running the Microsoft Windows OS, encrypting data and demanding Bitcoin ransoms. It affected over 230,000 computers in over 150 countries.

These incidents underscore the vast scale and profound impact of cybersecurity breaches.

Lessons Learned

Every cyber incident, however damaging, offers lessons that can guide future prevention strategies.

1. **Regular Updates**: The Equifax breach highlighted the importance of regular system updates and patching vulnerabilities promptly.

2. **Backup and Recovery**: WannaCry emphasized the significance of regular backups and having a robust recovery plan in place.
3. **Awareness and Training**: Many incidents reveal that breaches often stem from human error or oversight. Regular training can significantly mitigate these risks.

How a Consultant Could Make a Difference

Cybersecurity consultants possess the expertise and foresight that can be invaluable in preventing or mitigating such incidents.

1. **Proactive Risk Assessment**: Before the breach occurs, consultants can identify potential vulnerabilities, ensuring they are addressed timely.
2. **Tailored Security Strategies**: Consultants can devise security strategies specific to an organization's needs and infrastructure, strengthening its defense mechanisms.
3. **Post-Incident Analysis**: In the unfortunate event of a breach, consultants can help analyze the root cause, ensuring the organization learns and fortifies its defenses against future attacks.

Engaging a cybersecurity consultant isn't just about handling existing problems—it's about foreseeing potential threats and nipping them in the bud.

In conclusion, studying past cybersecurity incidents isn't about pointing fingers or dwelling on mistakes. It's a forward-looking exercise, drawing insights and strategies to better prepare for future challenges. A cybersecurity consultant stands at the juncture of this learning process, equipped to guide organizations through the complex labyrinth of digital security, ensuring they emerge stronger, smarter, and more resilient. As we progress further into our exploration, we will delve deeper into specialized tools and techniques that professionals use to protect and fortify the digital realm.

CHAPTER 11:

Future Trends in Cybersecurity

Rise of Quantum Computing and its Implications

The world stands on the cusp of a quantum revolution, and with it comes a new set of challenges and opportunities for cybersecurity.

1. **Enhanced Security**: Quantum encryption promises virtually unbreakable security. Quantum Key Distribution (QKD) ensures that any attempt to eavesdrop on a communication will disrupt the quantum state of the system, alerting the users.

2. **Potential Threats**: On the flip side, quantum computers can potentially break classical encryption methods in seconds. Systems that were once deemed secure could become vulnerable overnight.

3. **Transition Period**: As quantum computing becomes more prevalent, there will be a transition phase where both quantum and classical encryption methods co-exist, requiring a hybrid approach to cybersecurity.

The rise of quantum computing is a double-edged sword, promising unparalleled security while also posing new threats.

Increasing Automation in Cybersecurity

Automation is increasingly becoming the backbone of effective cybersecurity, responding to threats faster than any human could.

1. **Threat Detection**: Automated systems can sift through vast amounts of data, identifying potential threats or anomalies in real-time.

2. **Response Protocols**: Once a threat is detected, automated systems can initiate predefined response protocols, minimizing the damage.

3. **Reducing Human Error**: Automating repetitive tasks reduces the chance of human error, a leading cause of security breaches.

While automation boosts efficiency and responsiveness, it's essential to maintain a balance with human oversight to ensure nuanced decision-making.

The Role of AI and Machine Learning

Artificial Intelligence (AI) and Machine Learning (ML) are no longer just buzzwords—they're transforming cybersecurity.

1. **Predictive Analysis**: ML algorithms can analyze patterns and predict potential future threats, allowing for proactive defense measures.

2. **Behavior Analysis**: AI can study user behavior, flagging any deviation from the norm. This can quickly identify compromised accounts or insider threats.

3. **Adapting to New Threats**: Traditional security systems rely on known threat databases. AI and ML can adapt and learn from new threats, ensuring the system evolves with the ever-changing cybersecurity landscape.

The integration of AI and ML into cybersecurity promises a more adaptive and forward-thinking approach, but it's crucial to ensure these technologies are used ethically and responsibly.

In conclusion, the future of cybersecurity is an exciting blend of groundbreaking technologies and novel strategies. While new challenges will undoubtedly arise, so will innovative solutions. By understanding and harnessing these upcoming trends, cybersecurity professionals can ensure that they are always one step ahead, ready to protect and defend the digital realm. As our journey into the world of cybersecurity continues, we will explore even more facets, tools, and techniques, ensuring a comprehensive grasp of the field.

CHAPTER 12:

Building a Cybersecurity Practice

Structuring a Consultancy Business

Launching a successful cybersecurity consultancy requires more than technical expertise; it demands a strong foundation and a strategic business approach.

1. **Business Plan**: Start with a clear business plan, outlining your niche, target audience, financial projections, and growth strategies.
2. **Legal Framework**: Decide on the right business structure, be it sole proprietorship, partnership, LLC, or corporation. This decision impacts taxes, liability, and compliance regulations.
3. **Service Offerings**: Clearly define the services you're offering. This could range from vulnerability assessments and penetration testing to policy formulation and staff training.
4. **Operational Strategy**: Set up standard operating procedures (SOPs) to ensure consistency in service delivery, client interactions, and data management.

By putting a solid structure in place, you set the stage for a scalable and sustainable cybersecurity consultancy.

Collaborative Tools for Cybersecurity Teams

In the era of remote work and distributed teams, effective collaboration is paramount.

1. **Communication Platforms**: Tools like Slack or Microsoft Teams facilitate real-time communication and streamline project discussions.

2. **Project Management Tools**: Platforms such as Trello, Asana, or Jira help in task tracking, deadline management, and workflow visualization.

3. **Shared Documentation**: Cloud-based solutions like Google Drive or Dropbox allow teams to collaboratively work on documents, ensuring everyone is on the same page.

4. **Secure Virtual Meeting Platforms**: For client meetings or team briefings, opt for secure platforms with end-to-end encryption.

Selecting the right suite of tools is essential for fostering a cohesive team environment, even if team members are scattered across the globe.

Marketing and Client Acquisition Strategies

Building a client base is pivotal to your consultancy's success.

1. **Online Presence**: Invest in a professional website showcasing your services, case studies, and client testimonials. Pair this with an active presence on professional networks like LinkedIn.

2. **Content Marketing**: Share articles, videos, or webinars on latest cybersecurity trends. This positions you as an authority in the field and draws potential clients.

3. **Networking**: Attend industry conferences, seminars, and workshops. Personal connections often lead to referrals and long-term client relationships.

4. **Client Testimonials and Case Studies**: Displaying feedback from satisfied clients boosts credibility. Detailed case studies further illustrate the tangible value you bring.

To grow and sustain your cybersecurity consultancy, it's crucial to have a multifaceted approach to marketing, blending digital strategies with traditional networking.

In wrapping up, building a robust cybersecurity practice demands a blend of technical acumen, strategic planning, and business savvy. The landscape of cybersecurity is ever-evolving, and so too should your practice be, adapting to new challenges, technologies, and market demands. As you venture forth in establishing and expanding your cybersecurity consultancy, let this chapter serve as a foundational guide to propel you towards success

Conclusion

Reflection on the Changing Cybersecurity Landscape

As we draw this exploration of cybersecurity to a close, it's vital to take a step back and truly appreciate the vast and dynamic landscape we've navigated. The digital realm, once a frontier of uncharted potential, has now become an integral part of our daily lives. With its expansion has come an increasing array of threats, underscoring the ever-growing need for robust cybersecurity.

1. **Rapid Evolution**: The digital threats of yesteryears were vastly different from those we face today. We've transitioned from mere viruses and worms to intricate state-sponsored cyberattacks and ransomware campaigns.
2. **A Shift in Perception**: Cybersecurity, once seen as a mere IT concern, has now catapulted to boardroom discussions. Businesses and individuals alike recognize its value, with repercussions of neglect becoming evident in high-profile breaches.
3. **Interconnected Challenges**: Our hyper-connected world means that a vulnerability in one system can quickly cascade, affecting interconnected networks, emphasizing the importance of a holistic defense strategy.

The landscape's continuous change, while posing challenges, also offers opportunities for innovation, growth, and fortification against threats.

Encouraging Proactivity in Risk Management

If there's one key takeaway from this journey, it's the significance of being proactive rather than reactive when managing risks.

1. **Anticipate, Don't Just React**: By staying abreast of emerging threats and understanding the evolving digital landscape, one can preemptively strengthen defenses, reducing the likelihood of successful attacks.

2. **Continuous Learning**: Cybersecurity isn't a one-time effort. It demands continuous learning, training, and adaptation. The threats of tomorrow will differ from those of today, and preparedness is crucial.

3. **Empower and Educate**: Beyond just implementing tools and protocols, fostering a culture of cybersecurity awareness at all organizational levels is paramount. When everyone is vigilant, the collective defense is significantly more potent.

By embracing a proactive stance, we can transform risk management from a daunting task to an empowering strategy, ensuring not just survival but also thriving in the digital age.

In closing, while the challenges in cybersecurity are myriad, the tools, strategies, and insights shared in this book aim to arm you, whether a budding consultant or a concerned individual, with the knowledge to navigate them. As we continue our journey in the digital age, remember always to prioritize security, be proactive in your approach, and remain adaptable to the ever-changing cyber landscape.

Appendices

A: Glossary of Cybersecurity Terms

Cybersecurity, with its technical nature, comes with a myriad of terms that can be overwhelming. This glossary provides concise definitions for common and vital terms in the industry.

1. **Authentication**: The process of verifying the identity of a user or system.
2. **Authorization**: The process of granting or denying access to resources based on a user's identity.
3. **Botnet**: A network of compromised computers controlled by an attacker, often used for launching distributed denial-of-service (DDoS) attacks.
4. **Cryptography**: The science of using codes to secure information.
5. **DDoS (Distributed Denial-of-Service)**: An attack aimed at overwhelming a system with traffic, rendering it inaccessible.
6. **Encryption**: The process of converting information into a code to prevent unauthorized access.
7. **Firewall**: A network security device or software that monitors and filters incoming and outgoing traffic, blocking or allowing it based on security policies.
8. **Hacker**: An individual who exploits vulnerabilities in a system, either for malicious intent or for identifying security weaknesses.

9. **Intrusion Detection System (IDS)**: A device or application that monitors networks for malicious activity or policy violations.//
10. **Intrusion Prevention System (IPS)**: A system that not only detects malicious activities but also takes action to prevent them.
11. **Malware**: Malicious software designed to harm, exploit, or otherwise compromise a computer, network, or system.
12. **Phishing**: A cyberattack in which attackers disguise themselves as trustworthy entities to steal sensitive information like usernames or passwords.
13. **Ransomware**: Malware that encrypts a victim's files, with the attacker demanding payment in exchange for the decryption key.
14. **Secure Socket Layer (SSL)**: A protocol for establishing encrypted links between a web server and a browser, ensuring all data passed between them remains private.
15. **Two-Factor Authentication (2FA)**: An authentication method that requires two types of identification, usually a password and a secondary code sent to a device.
16. **Virtual Private Network (VPN)**: A technology that creates a secure, encrypted connection over a less secure network, such as the internet.
17. **Vulnerability**: A weakness in a system that could be exploited by an attacker.
18. **White-hat hacker**: Ethical hackers who break into systems to identify vulnerabilities, not to exploit them.
19. **Zero-day exploit**: A cyberattack that targets vulnerabilities unknown to those who would be interested in patching the vulnerability.

20. **Endpoint security**: The process of securing endpoints or entry points of end-user devices like computers, mobile devices, and more.

This glossary offers a foundational understanding of essential cybersecurity terms. As the cybersecurity landscape evolves, new terms and concepts continually emerge. It's beneficial for professionals and enthusiasts to stay updated on new terminologies.

B: Recommended Reading and Resources

Books:

a. **"The Art of Invisibility"** by Kevin D. Mitnick: Delve into strategies of staying digitally invisible and protecting personal information.

b. **"Cybersecurity and Cyberwar: What Everyone Needs to Know"** by P.W. Singer and Allan Friedman: A comprehensive overview of the cyber realm.

c. **"Future Crimes: Inside the Digital Underground and the Battle for Our Connected World"** by Marc Goodman: Learn about the digital threats of today and how they might evolve in the future.

d. **"Ghost in the Wires: My Adventures as the World's Most Wanted Hacker"** by Kevin D. Mitnick: A memoir detailing Mitnick's life as a hacker and his eventual transformation into a security consultant.

e. **"Countdown to Zero Day: Stuxnet and the Launch of the World's First Digital Weapon"** by Kim Zetter: An analysis of the Stuxnet worm and its implications in the world of cyber warfare.

Online Courses:

a. **"Introduction to Cybersecurity"** offered by Cybrary: A beginner's course discussing the foundational concepts of cybersecurity.

b. **"Computer and Network Hacker Techniques"** offered by Stanford Online: Dive deep into hacker techniques and how to counteract them.

c. **"Cybersecurity for Business"** by Coursera: This course is specifically designed for professionals looking to integrate cybersecurity practices into their business operations.

Blogs and Websites:

a. **Krebs on Security**: Run by journalist Brian Krebs, this site offers deep dives into current cybersecurity threats and news.

b. **The Hacker News**: A platform dedicated to discussing the latest in security, technology, and hacker news.

c. **Dark Reading**: Covers the latest cybersecurity news, threats, and trends.

Podcasts:

a. **"Smashing Security"**: A weekly podcast discussing the latest in cybersecurity with a touch of humor.

b. **"The CyberWire Daily"**: Stay updated with the latest cybersecurity news condensed into 20-minute episodes.

c. **"Darknet Diaries"**: True stories from the dark side of the internet. It delves into various hacks, data breaches, and cyber crimes.

Reports and Journals:

a. **The Verizon Data Breach Investigations Report (DBIR)**: An annual publication analyzing the latest patterns and trends in cybersecurity.

b. **Journal of Cybersecurity**: A peer-reviewed journal addressing key issues in cybersecurity from both technical and social perspectives.

These resources provide a diverse range of insights, from hands-on skills in cybersecurity to understanding the broader implications of cyber threats in our interconnected world. Whether you're a seasoned professional or just beginning, these materials can offer substantial value.

C: List of Important Cybersecurity Conferences and Forums

Networking and continuous learning are essential in cybersecurity. Here are the must-attend events:

1. **RSA Conference (RSAC)**: Held annually in San Francisco, this is one of the world's leading cybersecurity events.
2. **Black Hat USA**: A global event series providing attendees with the latest in research, development, and trends.
3. **DEF CON**: One of the oldest and most attended hacker conferences. It is held annually in Las Vegas.
4. **SANS Institute Conferences**: The SANS Institute hosts multiple events worldwide focused on IT and cybersecurity training.
5. **CyberTech**: The largest annual cybersecurity event outside of the U.S., held in Tel Aviv, Israel.
6. **ShmooCon**: An annual east coast hacker convention offering three days of an interesting atmosphere for demonstrating technology exploitation.
7. **Infosecurity Europe**: Europe's number one information security event, featuring Europe's largest conference program.
8. **HITB Security Conference**: Held in Amsterdam and Asia, this conference offers technical talks and discussions on groundbreaking attack and defense methods.
9. **CanSecWest**: Held in Vancouver, Canada, it's a venue for leading information security professionals to discuss their latest findings.
10. **Thotcon**: An annual event held in Chicago focusing on hacking, security, and innovative tech.
11. **DerbyCon**: Celebrates the intersection of technology, humans, and cybersecurity, and is held in Louisville, Kentucky.

12. **SecTor**: Canada's premier IT security conference, offering insights into the latest research and techniques.
13. **Kaspersky's Security Analyst Summit (SAS)**: Features top cybersecurity experts from global IT vendors, international organizations, and law enforcement agencies.
14. **TROOPERS**: An annual event held in Germany that delves deep into the world of IT security.
15. **AppSec USA**: A conference run by the Open Web Application Security Project (OWASP) focusing on application security.
16. **AusCERT**: The premier cybersecurity conference in Australia, offering attendees the chance to network with industry leaders.

While this list is comprehensive, there are countless other regional and specialized cybersecurity conferences around the world. Staying engaged with these events can be vital for professionals to remain updated on the latest trends, threats, and solutions in the cybersecurity realm.

D: Tools and Software Recommendations for Consultants

For consultants aiming to provide top-tier services, having the right tools is paramount. Here's a list of recommended software and tools:

1. **Vulnerability Assessment and Penetration Testing (VAPT):**

   - **Nmap**: An open-source tool for network exploration and security auditing.
   - **Metasploit**: A penetration testing platform that aids in finding, exploiting, and validating vulnerabilities.
   - **Burp Suite**: A tool for web vulnerability scanning and penetration testing.
   - **OWASP ZAP**: An open-source web application security scanner.
   - **Wireshark**: Network protocol analyzer used to capture and display the data traveling back and forth on a network in real-time.

2. **Endpoint Security:**

   - **CylancePROTECT**: Uses AI to prevent malware attacks.
   - **Malwarebytes**: Provides protection against malware, ransomware, and other advanced threats.
   - **Symantec Endpoint Protection**: Offers defense against all types of attacks for both physical and virtual systems.

3. **Firewall and Intrusion Detection/Prevention Systems (IDS/IPS):**

   - **Snort**: Open-source network intrusion prevention and detection system.
   - **Suricata**: High-performance network IDS, IPS, and network security monitoring.
   - **pfSense**: Open-source firewall and router software.

4. **Encryption and Privacy:**

- **TrueCrypt/VeraCrypt**: Disk encryption software to create encrypted virtual disks.
- **OpenSSL**: Toolkit for the Transport Layer Security (TLS) and Secure Sockets Layer (SSL) protocols.
- **GnuPG**: Free implementation of the OpenPGP standard, used for encrypting data and communication.

5. **Incident Response and Forensics**:

- **Volatility**: Advanced memory forensics framework.
- **The Sleuth Kit (TSK)**: Collection of UNIX and Windows-based utilities for forensic analysis.
- **Redline**: Provides host investigative capabilities to users for identifying malicious activities.

6. **Security Information and Event Management (SIEM)**:

- **Splunk**: Software for searching, monitoring, and analyzing machine-generated data.
- **ELK Stack (Elasticsearch, Logstash, Kibana)**: Open-source log management.
- **ArcSight**: Enterprise cybersecurity and risk management solution.

7. **Secure Coding and Static Analysis**:

- **Checkmarx**: Provides software security solutions for identifying, tracking, and repairing security flaws.
- **Fortify**: Static code analyzer offering continuous security.

8. **Password and Credential Management**:

- **LastPass**: Password manager that stores encrypted passwords online.
- **KeePass**: Free and open-source password manager.
- **Hashcat**: Advanced password recovery tool.

9. **Cloud Security**:

- **CloudSploit**: Scans AWS accounts for security configurations, helping to maintain a robust environment.
- **Barracuda Cloud Security Guardian**: Ensures compliance and auto-remediates security incidents within cloud services.

10. **Training and Simulation**:

- **GoPhish**: Open-source phishing toolkit used for phishing simulation training.
- **Hack The Box**: An online platform to test and advance penetration testing skills.

This list provides a solid foundation, but the tools a consultant should use depend largely on the specific needs and contexts of their clients. Regular updates and training are also essential, as the cybersecurity landscape is dynamic and continually evolving.

In conclusion, these appendices are designed to be a handy reference, assisting readers in navigating the intricate world of cybersecurity. Whether you're a seasoned professional or just beginning your journey, these resources will be invaluable as you aim to deepen your understanding and enhance your skills in the realm of cybersecurity.

Index

Note: The Index is organized alphabetically, allowing readers to easily locate specific topics, terms, and discussions covered in the book. The references are linked to the chapter numbers for easier navigation.

A

- Artificial Intelligence in Cybersecurity: Chapter 11
- Asset Management, Digital: Chapter 2
- Audits, Security: Chapter 5
- Authentication Mechanisms: Chapter 6

B

- Black Hat USA Conference: Chapter 9
- Blockchain and Cybersecurity: Chapter 11
- Breaches, Data: Chapter 10

C

- Case Studies in Cybersecurity: Chapter 10
- Cloud Security: Chapter 7
- Compliance, Regulatory: Chapter 8
- Conferences, Cybersecurity: Chapter 9
- Cryptography Basics: Chapter 6
- Cybersecurity Culture, Building a: Chapter 7

D

- Defense in Depth Strategy: Chapter 5
- DerbyCon Conference: Chapter 9
- Digital Assets: Chapter 2
- DDoS Attacks: Chapter 4

E

- Encryption:
- Data-at-rest: Chapter 6
- Data-in-transit: Chapter 6
- Ethical Considerations for Consultants: Chapter 9

F

- Firewalls: Chapter 6
- Forensics, Digital: Chapter 7
- Future Trends in Cybersecurity: Chapter 11

G

- Global Cybersecurity Standards: Chapter 8
- Glossary of Cybersecurity Terms: Appendices

H

- Hacking, Ethical: Chapter 4
- Human Factors in Cybersecurity: Chapter 7

I

- IDS/IPS Systems: Chapter 6
- Incident Response Planning: Chapter 5
- Insider Threats: Chapter 7
- Internet of Things (IoT) Security: Chapter 7

K

- Key Management: Chapter 6

L

- Legal Implications in Cybersecurity: Chapter 8

- Lifecycle, Risk Management: Chapter 3

M

- Machine Learning in Cybersecurity: Chapter 11
- Malware Types and Defense: Chapter 4

N

- Network Security Basics: Chapter 6

P

- Patch Management: Chapter 6
- Penetration Testing: Chapter 4
- Phishing Attacks: Chapter 4
- Portfolio, Building for Consultants: Chapter 9

Q

- Quantum Computing and Cybersecurity: Chapter 11

R

- Recommended Reading and Resources: Appendices
- Risk:
  - Assessment: Chapter 4
  - Management: Chapter 3

S

- Secure Coding Practices: Chapter 6
- Security Awareness Training: Chapter 7
- Social Engineering Attacks: Chapter 7
- Software Recommendations for Consultants: Appendices

T

- Tools for Cybersecurity Consultants: Appendices
- Two-Factor Authentication (2FA): Chapter 6

V

- Vulnerabilities, Identifying: Chapter 4

Printed in Great Britain
by Amazon